SECRET SWANSEA

Lisa Tippings

AMBERLEY

First published 2019

Amberley Publishing
The Hill, Stroud
Gloucestershire, GL5 4EP

www.amberley-books.com

Copyright © Lisa Tippings, 2019

The right of Lisa Tippings to be identified as the
Author of this work has been asserted in accordance
with the Copyrights, Designs and Patents Act 1988.

ISBN 978 1 4456 8866 4 (print)
ISBN 978 1 4456 8867 1 (ebook)

British Library Cataloguing in Publication Data.
A catalogue record for this book is available from the
British Library.

Origination by Amberley Publishing.
Printed in Great Britain.

Contents

Introduction

One of my earliest memories of Swansea is of making the journey with my family from the Welsh Valleys in the south, to the west's beautiful coastline. In 1970s Wales, many factories ended each July with a two-week shutdown, and across the industrial south the whir and grind of machinery gradually faded into a haze of sun-swept silence. As each conveyor belt and apparatus slowed to stoppage, the annual exodus of beleaguered families to the coast began.

My family would trundle in our purple Renault Estate along roads that twisted and twined their way to the coast, tarmac narrowed further still by the hedgerows that boxed in fields of sheep in the south, or more likely crops such as rapeseed to the west. Sometimes we stayed with the curve of tapered roads and made our way towards the Gower Coast and Port Eynon, where my grandmother sited her caravan. At other times, the thrill of Swansea Bay beckoned, and Dad would escape the tangle of minor roads at Neath and join the M4, our car huffing in protest at the unexpected gear change, before spluttering into a streak of purple. Mum's glance was one of anxiety, but Dad's smile was one of triumph as his foot flattened the accelerator to the floor of the car and with poorly concealed joy we left the interminable stop-start slowness of B-roads behind us.

If the creation of the M4 brought economic and cultural change to south Wales, it also ensured that Swansea's fate as a tourism hotspot was sealed. From its inception in the early 1960s, each stretch of newly placed motorway brought people south of London nearer to the west's coastline, meaning that, as it did so, the M4 was guaranteed to bring holidaymakers in need of sunshine and escape straight to Swansea's doorstep. This allowed the city to become a favourite not just with Welsh tourists and day trippers, but also with travellers from further afield, who for the first time had easy access to Swansea's tantalising mix of coast and countryside. However, from 1977 onwards, Swansea Bay was able to entice tourists to its shores with something other than the old-fashioned pleasures of a traditional seaside holiday.

Situated on what was once Victoria railway station, Swansea's newly built leisure centre had a swimming pool like no other in Wales. It came installed with a wave machine, meaning that at its most popular, around 800,000 visitors a year gulped and screamed their way through throngs of swimmers, all eager for their bodies to be swayed and then submerged by wave after wave of water. As a family, we too were anxious to experience technology and be half-drowned by chlorinated water, as opposed to walking half a mile further down the bay in order to enjoy the thrill of real salt water in our hair. The bemusement we felt at enjoying first-hand the most up-to-date technical wizardry momentarily took a shine off Swansea's golden coastline, but as queuing for car parking and changing rooms became as onerous as driving on B-roads, the call of real waves began to be heard. Before long our holidays found us heading once more to Swansea Bay, to icy-cold water and to grains of sand in our lunchtime picnic.

In 2003, after almost thirty years of constant wear and tear, Swansea Leisure Centre was closed for refurbishment. Five years later it was reopened by HRH Queen Elizabeth II, who christened it LC2. Now, twenty-first-century technology abounds in the surf simulator and water slides, but, for me, the pool will always be remembered for its fake waves, which thrilled the children of Wales in the 1970s and 1980s.

When I was a child, I loved Swansea because it gave me a chance to escape the humdrum of everyday life. I associated it with holidays from school, ice creams, wave machines and overnight stays in a cramped caravan. But since moving here six years ago, I have discovered another side to Swansea. It is a city filled with historical intrigue, literary heritage, culture and a powerful political movement. Indeed, it is a city with many secrets to divulge, if you only know where to search...

NB Swansea was not officially made a city until 1969. However, in order to avoid any confusion, I have made the decision to refer to it as a city throughout this book, regardless of the year.

The LC2.

The LC2.

Swansea Bay.

1. Murder and Mayhem

Swansea's seafront, rather like that of Llandudno to the north, is lined with attractive Victorian guesthouses, all of which are suggestive of quiet holidays spent by genteel families eager to be seen mixing with the polite society of nineteenth-century Britain. Fast forward 150 years, and it becomes apparent that some of the grandeur of these hotels has faded and tarnished – so that while several retain their proud façades, others have crumbled, or have, at the very least, become less aloof, enjoying new statuses as long-stay bed and breakfasts for out-of-town workers.

However, regardless of their appearances both then and now, several of the hotels lining the seafront's Oystermouth Road have intriguing social histories, and it is apparent that such buildings were important but unfortunately silent witnesses to some of the dreadful events that occurred inside their rooms. These were undoubtedly events that, had their nineteenth-century guests known about them, would have caused their delicate sensibilities great alarm.

A great deal of sorrow and sadness also casts a shadow of gloom across each and every one of the poor souls who, for whatever reason, lost lives in Swansea's past. Some have done so by their own hand, driven in a fit of despair to end the sorrow that they faced, while others have had their lives cruelly taken by those who put their own selfish needs above all else. These characters have become woven into the dark tapestry of Swansea's murky past.

A closer look at the city's past proves it is not just the seafront hotels that have a secret history. As a coastal resort, Swansea's shoreline often fell victim to smugglers and pirates. These desperate men and women frequently felt the need to employ immoral measures in order to make money, but such immorality came at the cost of human life, and Swansea's hidden history is rife with stories of men and women who gave their life to the sea in a futile bid to make their fortune, or at least put bread upon the table.

A Sad and Lonely Suicide

In 1819 a suicide took place in a Swansea pub, which, had more been known about it at the time, had the potential to steadily shake the very foundations of an already troubled literary family. Indeed, there are few scholarly families so intertwined as those of Byron, Shelley, Wollstonecraft and Godwin, yet few seem to recall how one of their members ended her life in great sorrow at the Mackworth Arms in High Street, Swansea.

Mary Wollstonecraft was arguably Britain's first feminist. She was a woman who tasked herself with bringing to the forefront of the national consciousness the need for debate on the role females were allowed to play within their social spheres. Shortly after the publication of her work *A Vindication of the Rights of Woman* in 1792, she began a relationship with the American, Gilbert Imlay. Imlay was a businessman, and the pair

The genteel hotels on the seafront at Oystermouth Road as they look today.

An aerial view of the craggy beach at Port Eynon.

met in Paris at a time of political unrest. Although Wollstonecraft was later referred to as Mrs Imlay, the couple never officially married, meaning that their daughter Francis, or Fanny as she was known, was illegitimate. Although Wollstonecraft still despaired at the notion of swearing obedience to any man, she was drawn to Imlay and felt comfortable with him. Indeed, in spite of the fact that Imlay's business ventures appeared to be so diametrically opposed to her own political and literary interests, Wollstonecraft's letters from the time suggest her intention to maintain their relationship, even if this appeared to further quash her own self-esteem.

Unfortunately, there is little doubt that Imlay quickly lost interest in the mother of his child and that he saw her as more of a hindrance than the help she sought to be. Even though she was willing to undertake a dangerous trip to Scandinavia, alone except for Fanny and a maid, all on his behalf, Imlay's attention was incapable of staying focussed on his common-law wife. By the mid-1790s he was heaping humiliation further on Wollstonecraft by living with another woman. In spite of having a child with Wollstonecraft he did nothing to hide his precarious domestic arrangements, and this only added further distress to her growing humiliation. Her desire for domestic harmony and equality, as outlined in *A Vindication of the Rights of Woman*, where she criticised the

Mary Wollstonecraft.

fact that 'Pleasure is the business of a woman's life, according to the present modification of society, and while it continues to be so, little can be expected from the first fair defect in nature...' seemed as far away as ever. Exhausted and scorned, Wollstonecraft left Fanny in the care of a maid and attempted to commit suicide by jumping from a secluded bridge over the River Thames. However, life was not done with Wollstonecraft just yet. She was spotted and rescued, and over the coming months while recovering she came to the painful conclusion that if her life was to continue with any sense of peace and fulfilment, Gilbert Imlay could no longer play any part in it.

Bliss Cut Short

It was while recuperating with friends in London that Wollstonecraft became reacquainted with the writer William Godwin, having met him some years previously at the home of a mutual friend. Although first impressions had not been particularly pleasing on either side, their later meetings were much more promising. Friendship turned to attraction and respect, feelings that were made obvious by the couple's decision to marry in March 1797, shortly after Mary discovered she was pregnant.

However, Mary and William's happiness was to be brutally cut short. While giving birth, Mary suffered from severe complications that eventually led to her death, and the life of one of Britain's first female radicals ended abruptly, with manuscripts unfinished and ideas left unformulated. Fortunately, her daughter, also named Mary, survived. As she grew up her intellect became obvious and later she would write the Gothic novel *Frankenstein*.

A Tangled Web

After the death of her mother, Fanny Imlay's future was less satisfactory. William Godwin continued in his role as stepfather, but made no secret of the fact that he felt his own daughter Mary achieved childhood successes that outshone those of Fanny. Fanny's situation was made worse not only by Godwin's second marriage in 1801 to Mary Jane Clairmont, meaning that she was now living with two parents of no blood relation, but also by her growing attachment to Shelley following his first visit to the Godwin household in 1814.

The tangled web that had already began to encroach upon family life was made worse when Fanny was sent to Laugharne, Pembrokeshire, to spend some time on the farm of her maternal grandfather, Edward John Wollstonecraft. Godwin hoped this holiday would help ensure the infatuation between Shelley and Imlay would cease. To his horror, something worse happened. While Fanny was away, Shelly transferred his affections to Mary, so that by the time of Fanny's return, the couple, along with Godwin's other stepdaughter Claire Clairmont, had escaped to Europe. Fanny must have been distraught when news of Shelley and Mary's affair reached her, even more so when, upon their return from Europe, they set up house together in London. Godwin was anxious that Fanny take his side, whereas Mary and Shelley expected her to become their advocate. Poor Fanny was left torn between two family members while also dealing with her own grief as a spurned lover.

Months passed. William Godwin, unable to spend within his means, fell further and further into debt. His eventual acceptance of Shelley came as a result of his belief that with his aristocratic links, Shelley could help alleviate some of his financial worries. But his reliance on Fanny as a go-between put tremendous strain on her. It is believed that this, along with her stepmother's admonishments and constant goading, left Fanny feeling depleted and depressed, particularly as Shelley was beginning to grow tired of Godwin's pleas for help.

In October 1816 Fanny travelled to Swansea – perhaps on her way to visit her grandfather's farm in Laugharne. Her journey was broken at the now demolished Mackworth Arms in Swansea. After retiring for the night Fanny was not seen alive again. When she failed to reappear the following morning, workers from the pub broke down her door, only to find her collapsed with a half-consumed bottle of laudanum by her side. Her suicide note read, 'I have long determined that the best thing I could do was put an end to the existence of a being whose birth was unfortunate, and whose life has only been a source of pain to those persons who have hurt their health in endeavouring to promote her welfare.' Fanny was only twenty-two years old, yet seemed to have lived through a lifetime of sorrow for one so young. Upon her death, Shelley was moved to write,

> Her voice did quiver as we parted,
> Yet knew I not that heart was broken
> From which it came, and I departed
> Heeding not the words then spoken.
> Misery – O Misery,
> This world is all too wide for thee.

Percy Bysshe Shelley

DID YOU KNOW?
Following an inquest into her death, no mention was ever made of Fanny Imlay committing suicide. This might be down to the fact that due to their wealth and influence her family managed to erase any evidence of suicide, or of who she really was, from official records.

No member of her extended family claimed Fanny Imlay's body. A suggestion has been made that her body was buried in a pauper's grave at St John's Church, High Street, Swansea. This church later became St Matthew's and held its final service on 28 March 2004. It now functions as a charity for the homeless. Records to support suppositions about her final resting place have proved impossible to track down.

No known image of Fanny Imlay exists. She has become a shadowy footnote and a woman marginalised to the outer limits of Wollstonecraft and Godwin family history.

The building that was once St John's Church – believed to be the burial place of Fanny Imlay.

The graveyard at St John's, now a charity for the homeless named after St Matthew.

Promise of Excitement

Perhaps one of Swansea's most bloodthirsty secrets involves the rather eclectic combination of a young chorus girl from Sunderland, a seafront hotel, and a beautiful but isolated coastal cove.

At the turn of the twentieth century, when she was just fifteen years old, Sutherland-born Mamie Stuart, impressionable and eager to seek her fortune, was attracted by the promise of excitement and fame that the life of a stage actress could offer. Having the opportunity to leave behind the restrictions of Victorian and Edwardian life, Mamie could easily be regarded as a flapper girl, eager to taste the independence that had been forbidden to the generation that immediately proceeded hers. Descriptions of her that were later circulated seem to hint that she fully embraced the freedom of the early part of the new century. For example, she wore her dark brown hair short and fashionably bobbed, her teeth were even and well-maintained, and she was often referred to as 'glamorous'. Strangely, although she spent her time touring the country and performing, it was when she returned home that she met and fell in love with the charismatic Sunderland-born George Shotton. A surveyor by trade, he was thirteen years Mamie's senior, and easily able to charm her with his confidence and swagger. By 1918 the couple were married and after spending time living in a variety of hotels and boarding houses, the couple settled in the ironically named Ty-Llanwydd (the Abode of Peace), an isolated house overlooking Brandy Cove, Caswell Bay, on the Gower Peninsula.

It is hard to imagine how this change of circumstances must have effected Mamie. She was used to the bright lights of the theatre, to applause and to attention. Most importantly, she was used to being surrounded by the bustle of theatre life. Now she was surrounded by nothing but the roar of the sea as it swept into the bay, and the echo of the wind as it buttressed the clifftops. Little is known about Mamie and George's life at Ty-Llanwydd. The few facts that remain, however, suggest not only that Mamie was unhappy, but also that she lived in fear. In a letter to her parents she wrote candidly about her husband, 'The man is not all there. I don't think I will live with him much longer. I am very much afraid of him. He has put me in a great big house and just comes and goes when he likes.'

By Christmas 1919, the couple seemed to have vanished. Post from Mamie's parents to their daughter was returned, marked simply, 'House closed'. The only clue could be found at a seafront hotel in Swansea. A male guest was recalled checking out in December, leaving behind him a large trunk. When the trunk had not been claimed by the following March, the police were informed. Upon opening the trunk, the attending officers found two dresses and a pair of shoes, all of which had chillingly been cut to ribbons. More importantly, alongside a Bible, a rosary and some jewellery, they also found a piece of paper bearing the name and address of Mamie Stuart's parents. Captain and Mrs Stuart

View from Caswell Bay cliffs.

were able to identify the possessions as belonging to Mamie and informed the police of their concerns regarding her safety, and also of their inability to contact her.

With alarm bells ringing about Mamie's safety, the police decided to investigate. Fearing the worst, they searched for George Shotton and were shocked by what they discovered. Shotton was living in yet another isolated abode – this time a cottage in Caswell Bay called Bonavista. However, he was not alone, but was living with his first wife May, whom he had married in 1905, and their child. Shotton protested his innocence and denied being a bigamist, claiming instead that he was merely an errant husband who had strayed but who had come to his senses when his mistress, Mamie, had been unfaithful. Some evidence appears to exist which hints at Mamie's possible infidelity. In his possession Shotton had a letter apparently written by Mamie to her lover where she claimed, 'I will be with you shortly and we can make up for lost time. My old man seems to know quite a lot, but what the eyes don't see the heart can't grieve for. Am just dying to see you and feel your dear arms around me.'

Jealous Rage

In spite of George Shotton's protestations, police remained highly suspicious, believing that on finding out about Mamie's possible infidelity, he had killed her in a fit of jealous rage and had possibly buried her body somewhere nearby. Unfortunately, an extensive search of grounds surrounding the cottage in which they had lived failed to uncover any evidence of foul play, so when Shotton faced the court in July 1920, he did so under the charge of bigamy and nothing more.

It was a case that captured the collective imagination of the nation. A charge of bigamy was sordid enough, but the added intrigue of Mamie's ongoing disappearance added further scandal to the story. It was just the sort of drama post-war Britons needed to take their minds off the daily grief and sorrow that otherwise faced them.

On Monday 31 May 1920, the *Sunderland Daily Echo* reported: 'George Shotton, aged 40, described as a marine superintendent, of Penarth, was charged on remand at Swansea on Saturday with bigamy, having it alleged, on March 25th, 1918, married Mamie Stuart at the Registry office South Shields, during the lifetime of his wife, Mary Shotton, whom he married at the parish church at St Woolos, Newport, on September 7th, 1905.' But certainly her many friends and family in Sunderland continued to fear for Mamie's life. The report continues, 'Her relatives who live in the west end of the town, have of course been anxious as to her whereabouts for the past six months, but all efforts they have made to trace her have failed. They very much fear that she is no longer alive.' But with no further evidence against him, other than the charge of bigamy, there was nothing that either the police or Mamie's family could do. The court ordered that George Shotton be sentenced to eighteen months' hard labour and that sadly seemed to be the end of the matter. Captain and Mrs Stuart died without knowing what happened to their daughter. Upon being released from prison, George Shotton led something of an itinerant life, until settling for some time near Tintern, where he ran a smallholding. He died in Bristol, penniless and alone, three years before his life hit the headlines once again.

In 1961, three youngsters from Swansea began to explore a disused lead mine at Brandy Cove. There they made a discovery that finally gave some peace to those members of

Mamie's family who still pondered over her whereabouts. Hidden within the walls of the mine they found the remains of a skeleton. Local police later discovered not only had the body been callously sawn into three, but that the remaining possessions found with the remains did indeed belong to Mamie Stuart.

After forty years the case of Mamie Stuart's disappearance was finally closed, and her family could sleep soundly knowing that although it was too late for justice to be served, they knew, once and for all, what had happened to their glamorous and independent relative.

Caswell Bay looking towards Brandy Cove.

2. He Who Dares, Smuggles

A closer look at the city's past proves it is not just the seafront hotels that have a murky hidden history. As a coastal resort, Swansea's shoreline often fell victim to smugglers and pirates. These desperate individuals frequently felt the need to employ immoral measures in order to make money, but such immorality came at the cost of human life, and Swansea's hidden history is rife with stories of men and women who gave their life to the sea in a futile bid to make their fortune, or at least put bread upon the table.

Smuggling

In the twenty-first century, smuggling has become synonymous with drugs, alcohol and cigarettes, personal addictions that are far from vital to an individual's survival. Television documentaries show how those who smuggle are often forced into doing so by corrupt gangs, whose members are eager to take advantage of those less fortunate than themselves. The drugs that are smuggled do nothing but cause misery and hardship for thousands of people, and so there is no respect given to such mindless greed.

However, smuggling was not always based on individual greed. Although always illegal, the smuggling of goods was often the only way the poor working classes could strike a blow against their constant oppression at the hands of callous and greedy bosses who worked them to death for a few shillings and pence.

In the eighteenth and nineteenth centuries, Swansea Bay and the Gower Peninsula were perfect places for those smugglers keen to exploit the coastline's secret nooks and crannies. Indeed, they were seen as ideal beaches on which to bring contraband ashore. Places such as Pennard, Pwll Du and the Salt House at Port Eynon have always been wild and rugged, and in their isolation provided the secrecy necessary to the gangs of men, willing to risk their lives in order to feed communities of people exhausted from facing years of starvation and neglect. However hard the customs men were willing to work in order to catch the bootleggers red-handed, the smugglers were determined to work even harder in order to evade capture.

One reason for the success of the Swansea smugglers is due in no small part to the power they yielded. Reports from the time claim that when they were due to illicitly import contraband into Swansea's harbour, they made arrangements for the customs men who were due on duty that day to receive requests to attend for jury service. The question this provokes is an interesting one. How did a group of apparently lawless, working-class men and women manage to infiltrate the higher echelons of society to the point where they were successful in corrupting the incorruptible and persuading the authorities to not only turn a blind eye to their criminal behaviour, but to also help support it?

The answer may lie in looking at the hierarchy of the smuggling gangs themselves. Although predominantly comprised of men and women who were disenfranchised due

Port Eynon.

to ill-treatment and poverty, at the head of such groups there was invariably positioned someone of power and status. Among several such people in Swansea was John Lucas, a member of one of the most influential families in the area.

The Lucas Family

The Lucas family enjoyed a rich and privileged ancestry, as well as a heritage filled with royal connections. Sir Charles Lucas had been a royalist who fought on the side of Charles I in the English Civil War. He was executed by the Roundheads at Colchester in June 1661.

Unlike Sir Charles, however, John Lucas was a rebel, one who was never more content than when he was causing trouble for those in authority. But although he was quick with his fist, and thought nothing of throwing himself into brawls and skirmishes aplenty, his rebellious nature did not prevent him from coming to the aid of the poorer communities whose members made their home in Swansea and the Gower Peninsula.

Today, all that remains of the Salt House in Port Eynon lies in ruins, but several hundred years ago, the Salt House provided John Lucas with a lucrative business. Legend has it that it was built for him by his father David, in order that he could take advantage of the need for salt to flavour food and of the flourishing industries that often grew up around such coastal based businesses. Salt from the sea was extracted following a water evaporation process. This involved heating the water via coal power and then leaving the salt in large crates until it was completely dry. If the salt business proved to be profitable, Lucas

Pwlldu.

An aerial view of Port Eynon.

became aware of another business with which he could also furnish his pockets, while at the same time helping those members of the local community who were struggling to feed their families. He believed it was a business that could provide him with some much needed excitement ... smuggling.

Both the Salt House and Culver Hole (a medieval dovecote whose name is believed to originate from *culufre*, the Old English word for 'pigeon' or 'dove') provided places from which to smuggle goods, as well as to store them until the time was right to distribute them before they could be spotted by the customs men. Culver Hole, a cave-like structure that looms out of the side of a cliff overlooking Port Eynon, is surrounded by legend. One of these legends is that a labyrinth of secret passageways run from the cave to the Salt House, thus enabling John Lucas and his gangs of smugglers to move goods safely and secretly between each site. Smugglers even used the church at Port Eynon to store goods – it is believed barrels of alcohol were stored behind the altar. The sand dunes on the beach itself also played their part, hiding smuggled goods that were buried deep beneath their surface. Just like Swansea itself, the coast could appear to be one thing on the surface, but something completely different beneath.

William Arthur was another successful smuggler who employed gangs of working-class men, all based on Swansea's coast, to help him evade the infamous customs men and smuggle goods to shore. Arthur's men became rather heroic in their attempts to fight off the figures who represented authority, joining forces in great number when the need arose in order to vanquish the challenge posed by the customs men. Arthur's men were also wily in their attempts to hide the goods that had been smuggled, and their knowledge of local coves, nooks and crannies was invaluable when they needed to outwit

The Salt House.

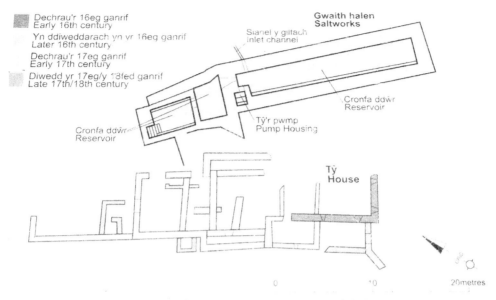

Map of the Salt House as it originally looked.

Artist's impression of how the Salt House originally looked.

Statue to remember those lost at sea, situated at the church at Port Eynon.

those who tried to usurp them. William Arthur ruled supreme in the latter decades of the eighteenth century, before finally giving up his 'job' as a smuggler and embracing the peace of legitimacy. He finally decided to give up his life as a rogue and found peace as a canal owner – no doubt employing some of the men who had previously helped him when he had been on the wrong side of the law!

The church at Port Eynon.

An aerial view of the Salt House.

The footpath the smugglers would have taken in order to reach the sand dunes at Port Eynon.

The sand dunes at Port Eynon.

3. Stalwarts of the Suffrage Movement

The fight for female emancipation was a long and hard-won battle fought by thousands of women who were determined to ensure they received not only parity at the polling station, but also equality at home and at work. For some women, it came at the cost of family life. There were those who found themselves disinherited by a patriarchal older generation who felt comfortable with the status quo and with the belief that men knew best. Other women found themselves made unappealing to future husbands simply because they had a viewpoint of their own that they believed in expressing in public. What linked all these women together was that from wherever they hailed in the British Isles, they were united by a common belief in equality between the genders.

However, a flick through any history book often gives the impression that only English women were at the forefront of the female fight for independence. Names such as Emmeline Pankhurst, Christabel Pankhurst and Emily Wilding Davison plaster the pages of books dedicated to the cause of female suffrage, perhaps misleading readers into believing that the fight for female emancipation was a very English affair. This could not be further from the truth; two of the leading lights in the Welsh suffrage movement lived and worked in Swansea.

A Different Approach

One of the reasons why the Welsh women who took part in the suffrage movement are often overlooked is because their approach was, in many ways, different from the one favoured by women such as Emmeline Pankhurst. While the Pankhursts and Emily Wilding Davison believed in direct action and in garnering attention for their cause through acts of violence against property, many women from Wales decided a different approach suited their needs better. One of the most important reasons for this was the economic climate that existed for many families in Wales at the time. A majority of the women who were willing to participate in the movement for equality in Wales came from poor socio-economic backgrounds. They could not afford to be locked away for damaging public property, however important to them the issue might be. They were needed at home, and females of all ages were expected to contribute in some way to the economy of the household, or to look after the younger children. Failure to do so could lead to extreme financial hardship, and this would be no more apparent than in some of the poorer coastal villages in and around Swansea, as well as in the city centre itself.

The majority of women in Swansea followed the pattern that was set by women in the rest of Wales and joined either the National Union of Women's Suffrage Societies (NUWSS) or the Women's Freedom League (WFL). Initiated by the English suffragist

Millicent Fawcett, the NUWSS was a society for moderate suffragists who believed that the violent actions of the suffragettes would harm their cause and turn the government against them, as opposed to drawing them towards their cause. Members made speeches, wrote letters and went on marches, but never attempted to behave in a way that was perceived as violent. The Women's Freedom League began in 1907, mainly as a reaction by more moderate members to the violent tactics employed by Emmeline Pankhurst's Women's Social and Political Union (WSPU). Others felt that her leadership was simply too autocratic.

Emily Phipps

Although not born in Wales, Emily Phipps spent a large part of her working life in Swansea, where, as the head teacher of Swansea Municipal Secondary Girls' School, she hoped to instil in the girls she taught a love of independence, a sense of pride and an appreciation of the value of equality. Before her arrival at the school it had a reputation for sending ill-informed and roughly educated girls out into the community, but after Emily Phipps' arrival she ensured this would never happen again. Her mission was to ensure that the young girls under her care were taught to make the most of their potential and to cherish and value the knowledge that a good education could offer them.

While dedicating her working life to the school, Emily still found time to use her free time profitably. After listening to the suffragist and WFL member Charlotte Despard make a speech in Swansea, at which she was heckled by gangs of men from the surrounding area, Emily became more determined than ever to participate in the growing movement for social change. Along with the support of another head teacher, Clara Neal, and a local woman called Mary Cleeves, Emily set up the Swansea branch of the WFL. It became one of the most successful WFL branches and inspired Emily to take part in a boycott that many women and liberal-minded men hoped would at last help to bring about the social change for which they fought.

Boycotting the Census

One of the strategies used by members of the WFL and other women in Swansea and beyond to draw attention to their fight for equality was to boycott the 1911 census. The reason behind this was both clear and rational. If, as women, they were not allowed to vote, they argued, why on earth should they agree to participate in a census requested by the government. Emily Phipps's beliefs were in accordance with this, and she wholeheartedly supported the motto used by suffragists at the time to persuade women to join their campaign. 'No votes, no census!' became a rallying cry for comradeship and many women were encouraged to 'disappear' on the night of the census so that their details could not be recorded. What makes Emily Phipps's contribution to the cause so special is the place she chose to hide herself away. Along with several other members of the WFL, she spent what must have been an exceptionally cold and uncomfortable night in a cave on the Gower Peninsula. As the sun rose, so did she and her fellow suffragists. Ignoring what must have been a very uncomfortable night, they simply returned to work. Proof, if it was needed, that women were capable of being as strong and bold as the men they were compared against so ill favourably.

Emily Phipps spent the rest of her life dedicating herself to promoting causes that helped women live fuller and more rewarding lives. She began by standing for Parliament in 1918 – the first time women were allowed to do so – and joined the National Federation of Women Teachers in order to campaign for equal rights for both female teachers as well as female students. Her death in 1943 brought to an end the life of a woman who had enriched the lives of so many other females, either because of her teaching or through her tireless campaign work. It is little wonder that today she is honoured by a blue plaque in the spot where Swansea Municipal Girls' School once stood.

DID YOU KNOW?
In the summer of 2017 Swansea Central Women's Institute commissioned a play about Emily Phipps. It was written by Sam O'Roarke and performed as part of the city's Troublemakers festival.

Amy Dillwyn

Emily Phipps was not the only campaigning suffragist in Swansea. Amy Dillwyn was also a fervent supporter of women's rights, as well as a novelist and one of Britain's first female industrialists. Like Emily Phipps, she was intelligent and tenacious, accomplishments that were not always prized in women in an era that expected its females to be subservient nurturers and family caregivers.

Unlike Emily Phipps, Amy Dillwyn was born in 1845 into a family of extreme privilege. As a Liberal MP for Swansea, Amy's father was heavily involved in the world of politics, and his father, Lewis Weston, owned the prestigious Sketty Hall. To a certain extent onlookers might have expected young Amy to grow up with a heavy weight of marital expectation on her shoulders. After all, mid-nineteenth-century Britain was not the best place to be if you were a woman seeking emancipation. It was instead a period heavily influenced by duty, and as the daughter of a wealthy, well-respected family, the onus would have been on Amy to agree to a suitable marriage regardless of the cost to her own personal happiness. Fortunately for Amy, the Dillwyns were nothing if not unconventional.

Brought up firstly in Parkwern, and then later in Hendrefoilan, Swansea, Amy and her siblings enjoyed a freedom that was not typically given to children of their age and status. Amy was allowed to question, and was allowed to be seen as well as heard, and there is little doubt that this sowed within her the seeds of freedom that would later play such an important part in her life. Amy was not a typical beauty either, most certainly not by conventional Victorian standards. She wore glasses and indeed paid little personal heed to her appearance, being more concerned with cultural matters or the politics of the day.

A plaque commemorating Amy Dillwyn.

The imposing Sketty Hall and Park as it is today.

In spite of this Amy became engaged at the age of eighteen to Llewellyn Thomas, an old school friend of her brothers. But their happiness was not to last as her fiancé died from smallpox before the marriage could take place. Amy was now seen as the spinster daughter of a wealthy Swansea family and thus certain expectations were finally put upon her. It was felt only right that she 'do her bit', and open charity sales of work and sell raffle tickets, although her sensitive nature made her rightly question this. She realised that many people she sold tickets to could barely afford the ticket price, yet they parted with their money simply because it was a Dillwyn who was offering them for sale. This made her feel hugely uncomfortable, even more so when three years later her mother died. As well as mourning for her parent, Amy was now left with little choice. As the only daughter at home it was incumbent upon her to play the role of lady of the house, however much she disliked it. What she feared most was the general futility of her role – that she was achieving so little when she was capable of achieving so much.

A Novel Idea

An important activity saved Amy Dillwyn from sinking into a deep depression, and also helped to distinguish her as a woman far ahead of her time. Her novel writing helped Amy to overcome any thoughts she might have harboured about an inability to embrace her full potential. Although her first attempt was rejected, Amy's tenacious personality refused to accept failure and in spite of the literary world being a male-dominated one, her second novel, *The Rebecca Rioter*, became her first to be published. Amy's novels gave her an opportunity to explore ideas, both social and political, and to highlight the facets of her own personality that were forbidden to her in her role as Amy Dillwyn, the munificent Swansea lady. She enjoyed delving into those aspects of her life that she was otherwise forced to keep hidden. In *Jill*, believed to be the novel that touches most on her true beliefs and innermost feelings (published in 1885), she considers the close friendship that can exist between two young women. This can be seen as reflecting her own feelings, although unreciprocated in a romantic sense, for her own close friend and distant relative Olive Talbot. Late nineteenth- and early twentieth-century Britain was not ready to comprehend romantic relationships between people of the same gender. This doubtless stifled a huge part of Amy Dillwyn's personality, but at least through the literature she published she had an opportunity to explore such feelings and to contemplate their impact on individuals who felt the same as she did.

Perhaps the biggest challenge Amy Dillwyn was forced to face occurred after her father's death in the early 1890s. Her only brother had died in 1890, meaning that Amy was now essentially homeless. The heir to her father's state was her nephew John Nicholl. Shortly, Amy would be forced to leave Hendrefoilan – the only home she could properly remember – and find her own accommodation.

Mary Dillwyn.

Her father, Lewis Dillwyn, believed that after his death his daughter Amy would be left relatively well off. After all, in his will he bequeathed her the Spelter works he owned in Llansamlet, Swansea. But Lewis Dillwyn was more of a politician than an industrialist and, preoccupied as he was with the politics of Swansea, he failed to realise that the Spelter works were being badly managed and that the accounts were in disarray. Although he intended to leave his daughter comfortably well-off, Amy was left nothing other than bills to pay and facing a worrying amount of debt.

Saving the Spelter Works

Lesser individuals might have crumbled when faced with the death of a parent, losing a home and inheriting nothing other than debt, but not Amy Dillwyn. She knew that if she simply got rid of the Spelter works, hundreds of Swansea locals would lose their jobs at a time when employment was difficult to come by. She refused to let this happen and in an era when women were meant to confine themselves to house and home, Amy rolled up her sleeves and set about finding ways to make the Spelter works thrive.

It is to her credit that she was successful. Not only was she able to satisfy her creditors, but she was also able to secure the future of the works, ensuring that not only did it begin to turn a profit, but that hundreds of jobs could be salvaged at the same time. If she initially shocked the people of Swansea then they soon got used to her eccentricities, particularly as she was giving so much back to her community. Success in a predominantly man's world gave her the confidence to flourish as the woman she was always meant to be. She openly began to smoke cigars, dress in the plain, androgynous attire that appealed to her bold nature, and was a continual source of inspiration to local suffragists, whose meetings she regularly attended.

When she died in 1935, she did so knowing that the ninety years she had spent on earth had been spent challenging the conventions enforced on women by a patriarchal society. She also knew that she had done all she could to help the women of Swansea and beyond have the courage to be true to themselves and to fight for the emancipation and equality she was convinced they deserved.

DID YOU KNOW?
Amy Dillwyn wrote seven published works, including *Jill* and its sequel, *Jill and Jack*. Amy Dillwyn's aunt, Mary Dillwyn, is believed to have been the first female photographer in Wales. As early as the 1840s she began taking photographs of the natural world, as well as children and family and friends. A pub in Fforest-fach, Swansea, has been named in her honour.

The Mary Dillwyn Pub, named after the first female photographer in Wales.

4. At the End of the Song Comes Payment

Wales is a country that, over the centuries, has become enriched by its literary heritage. From the earliest oral traditions of the *Mabinogion*, to the entrants shortlisted for the Welsh Book of the Year Award, where prizes are given to those who write in both English and Welsh, Wales has been blessed with some of the finest writers of any given era. While poetry lovers have been swept away by the works of R. S. Thomas, Danny Abse and Gillian Clarke, admirers of creative non-fiction have been captivated by the memoirs of Horatio Clare and Owen Sheers. Each span of centuries has ensured that Wales can offer something tantalising to tempt even the most resistant of readers.

Swansea has played a particularly important role in Wales's growing literary and cultural scene, and the list of writers and poets associated with the city and the Gower Peninsula keeps on growing. Perhaps the most famous of all, however, remains Dylan Thomas.

Cwmdonkin Drive

Every year thousands of visitors travel to the small town of Laugharne, on the south coast of Carmarthenshire, a journey that they take as part of their pilgrimage dedicated to the life of the poet, writer and broadcaster Dylan Thomas. Comfortably camouflaged by long grasses on a bank made safe by a slate wall, its windows overlooking the River Taf, stands the writer's 'Boathouse' – his writing shed only a few minutes' walk away, hidden by a turn in the road. The writing shed, kept as it is believed Thomas himself would have left it, has walls decorated with prints and cards and a floor strewn with crumpled balls of paper. It is here that the poet did indeed write some of his most famous works including 'Do Not Go Gentle', 'Over Sir John's Hill' and *Under Milk Wood*. However, in simply visiting Laugharne and its Boathouse, those who appreciate Dylan Thomas's poetry are missing out on one of the most important and formative places in his life, and a place that had a profound effect on his development both as a man and as a poet. The place in question is, of course, No. 5 Cwmdonkin Drive, Swansea, where in 1914 Dylan Thomas himself was born.

Cwmdonkin Drive is situated in the Uplands area of Swansea. The house was new when the Thomas family moved into it in 1914, and the interior bears testament to what it was really like to experience Welsh suburban living at the start of the twentieth century. The front parlour, or the 'best room', would surely have been saved for the most special of family occasions, such as Christmas and birthday meals, with the main everyday living being done in the sitting room and kitchen, both kept warm by the kitchen hob and grate. However, Dylan was not allowed to participate in any of life's everyday frivolities until his day's homework was complete and ready to be handed in to his schoolmaster the

Dylan Thomas's writing shed in Laugharne.

The Boat House.

Dylan Thomas's house on Cwmdonkin Drive.

following day. His father, David John Thomas, was a grammar school teacher and if he was strict with the students he taught, he was even stricter with his own son. He expected Dylan to excel academically, and playtime was reserved for those hours when schoolwork had been completed. This must have been particularly harsh on the young Dylan as the Thomas house overlooked Cwmdonkin Park, a favourite place of escape for the children in the area.

Although the best bedroom was spacious, with views overlooking Cwmdonkin Park, Dylan's bedroom was the smallest in the house. It was pokey and dark, leaving him little space to store all the possessions that a boy holds dear. But to compensate, the family was one of the lucky ones in that they were blessed with an indoor bathroom, and legend has it that as he grew older one of Dylan's favourite past-times was to lie in the bath puffing on a woodbine or two.

In spite of his cramped sleeping arrangements, and despite his youth, Dylan Thomas's literary output flourished while he lived in No. 5 Cwmdonkin Drive. While still only young, from here he was inspired to write stories and poems that in later life would create a backdrop from which he could explore the themes of beauty and nature, ideas that dominated so many of his poems and short stories.

View inside Cwmdonkin Park.

A map at the entrance to Cwmdonkin Park.

Swansea and the Gower Peninsula continued to inspire Dylan Thomas' literary output no matter where he was living or working. Cwmdonkin Park remained a source of inspiration, and his poem 'The Hunchback in the Park', about a man who is isolated from society due to his physical impairment, is heavily influenced by events Dylan saw and experienced for himself at the park. Despite being teased and goaded by the local children, the hunchback has nowhere else to stay, so spends his time in the park,

> Eating bread from a newspaper
> Drinking water from a chained cup.

Dylan writes that the hunchback drinks from the same 'fountain basin' as he had used as a place in which to sail his boats, and the truly autobiographical nature of the poem is fully reinforced for the reader.

Similarly, in his short story *Patricia, Edith and Arnold*, Dylan is undoubtedly 'The small boy in his invisible engine...' waiting to be taken to the park. Here the reader is given a glimpse into the imagination the young Dylan Thomas exhibited as a child, and also an opportunity to share his more than mischievous side. While Patricia the maid is otherwise occupied, the young boy, dressed neatly in his suit, scrambles into the coal shed, envisioning himself as 'King of the Coal Castle'. Only when he has failed to get Patricia's attention, in spite of several attempts at shocking her, 'I'm lying on my face in the coal,' does he resort to bad language: 'You'd better come soon,' the boy said, 'I'm dirty as Christ knows what.' In spite of her admonishments, it is clear that Patricia is still fond of the little rogue who has been placed in her care, and perhaps this story, more than any other, gives a glimpse into the true essence of Dylan Thomas's character. He may have been reckless with money, found fidelity difficult, and turned far too often to alcohol when in need of comfort, but there was a side to him that inexorably drew people to him, and there is little doubt that this is what helped him when his life became the tangled web of trouble he so often found himself facing.

DID YOU KNOW?
It is possible not only to visit No. 5 Cwmdonkin Drive, but to also stay the night in one of the bedrooms and experience living as the Thomas family did just over a hundred years ago.

Visitors can tour the house as well as stay for the sort of traditional Welsh tea that would have been served in 1914 Wales.

A memorial to Dylan Thomas near Swansea Castle.

Harri Webb

Harri Webb is known as a poet, a Welsh nationalist and a librarian, with ideas that were so radical at the time he implemented them in the 1960s that they derived scorn as much as they fostered admiration. He is often associated with the Welsh Valleys, having spent a large chunk of his life living in a commune in Merthyr and working in Mountain Ash and Dowlais. However, he was born and indeed died in Swansea, and is buried in a grave overlooking Pennard Beach in Gower.

Harri Webb was born in 1920 and spent the first two years of his life in Ty Coch Road, Swansea, before the family moved to the predominantly working-class area of Catherine Street, near the city centre. Surrounded as he was by ordinary everyday workers as he grew up, Harri Webb's political beliefs would undoubtedly have been influenced by the rough and tumble of poverty and the struggle to make ends meet, which he was able to witness throughout the formative years of his life. His background ensured he was entitled to try for a scholarship, which he won, thus securing a place for himself at Oxford University. But it is difficult to understand how successful a period in his life this was. Few mentions of his academic studies at Oxford can be sourced in his writings. Whether from unhappiness or discomfort at having at having attended a university whose perceived

St Mary's Church, Pennard.

snobbery would later be at odds with his social and nationalist leanings, it is difficult to ascertain. What is clear is that his mother died during his time at Oxford, and this might have resulted in him not fulfilling his true academic potential. On the other hand, it might simply have been that perhaps by the late 1930s and early 1940s his political and social beliefs had begun to mean more to him than his academic achievements.

During the Second World War, Webb served as a translator, making good use of the languages he had studied at Oxford. The end of the war saw him return once more to Swansea, before a move to Merthyr Tydfil precipitated the period of his life for which he is most well known. He resided in Garth Newydd, a house that was shared by, among others, several pacifists and Meic Stephens, the creator of *Poetry Wales* and later the director of the Welsh Arts Council.

Libraries and LPs, Periodicals and Pamphlets

Harry Webb was nothing if not innovative in his approach to his library work. Since their inception in the nineteenth century, libraries and reading rooms in south Wales had tended to be dominated by the miners and factory workers, all male, for whom they had, in the main, been built. Although women used the libraries, the newspapers and magazines that sat snugly on the desks of the reading rooms were all aimed specifically at men. The rooms themselves smelled of tobacco and woodbines and in no way encouraged either women or the younger generation to enter the wood-panelled interiors of such closely guarded sanctums. Harri Webb, however, had an eye on the development of the future generation. What better way to entice young people into the library than by offering them the possibility of borrowing LPs they could otherwise ill afford? Libraries have remained a vital part of overcoming poverty for all generations of people from all over south Wales, Swansea included, and it was typical of the working-class, Swansea-born Harri Webb to have a firm understanding of this. Similarly, he also recognised that the position of women in the 1960s was also on the cusp of another social change. They were rightly demanding more from their lives and libraries were the ideal places to begin their learning journey and strike another blow for equality. So, filled with optimism about the part libraries could play in their future, Harri Webb also ensured that the reading rooms and shelves of the libraries he worked at (including one in Mountain Ash) were stocked with journals and novels that would attract a wider female membership through their doors. Not everyone was pleased with Harri Webb's decision to change some aspects of the libraries that he worked for, fearing perhaps that such modernisation would change forever the make-up of the library service to which they had become accustomed. Harri Webb was in no way daunted by this. He was a determined man, who knew what was needed in order to bring the libraries of the Welsh Valleys up to date.

Published Work

As well as working for the library service, Harri Webb was busy writing and publishing poetry and political articles. Some of his most notable works of poetry include 'The Green Desert', 'A Crown For Branwen' and 'Rampage and Revel'. In *No Half-Way House*, the reader can explore a selection of political writings in which Webb discusses his socialist leanings as well as his Welsh nationalism. His book *A Militant Muse* gives readers an opportunity to read examples of the many articles and essays Webb dedicated to Welsh culture and his dissatisfaction with aspects of Wales's position on a wider cultural spectrum.

His final poetry book was published in 1983. *Poems and Points* is generally believed to have marked the end of Harri Webb's poetry-writing career. He sadly suffered a stroke in 1985 and moved into a nursing home in Swansea, where he died in 1994. His legacy is one of great importance. He was not just a poet, but a man who used his job as a librarian to try to change the lives of those who lived in the Valleys. He was also a cultural commentator, proud of his Welsh roots, but at the same time not afraid to be critical when he felt that was what was called for. His love of Swansea is perhaps illustrated by the fact that he returned to the city in order to spend whatever time he had left to him in the place in which he had been born and had spent his childhood. Indeed, this is an idea that appears to be reflected in his obituary, which appeared in *The Independent* shortly after his death: 'But ever a "Swansea Jack," he asked to be moved to his home town, wanting I believe, to die there.' *The Independent*'s obituary also makes reference to Harri Webb's passion for all things Welsh and by extension, therefore, all things associated with his home city, commentating, 'The social condition of Wales was the "one theme, one preoccupation" of all his writing, though he set it in a broad frame of cultural allusion and contemporary significance.' Perhaps it is only fitting that the last few words in this section should belong

The graveyard at St Mary's Church.

St Mary's Church, Pennard.

to Harri Webb himself. There is no better way to show that this Swansea-born poet was determined that his poetry would always be accessible to the ordinary everyday people he grew up with in St Catherine Street, near the heart of the city centre.

Women of Fishguard
The Emperor Napoleon
He sent his ships of war
With spreading sails
To conquer Wales
And land on Fishguard shore
But Jemima, she was waiting
With her broomstick in her hand
And all the other women, too,
To guard their native land.
For the Russians and the Prussians
He did not give a damn
But he took on more than he bargained for
When he tried it on with Mam.

DID YOU KNOW?

There are several different theories given as to the origin of the term 'Swansea Jack'. Some believe the name stems from the many sailors who travelled from the port of Swansea, earning themselves the nickname Swansea Jack along the way.

Swansea tin was often made into the lunchboxes used by the miners who worked in the pits in and around Swansea. The nickname given to such lunchboxes was 'Jacks', hence the nickname Swansea Jack.

Jack, and thereafter, Swansea Jack, was also the name of the dog who became famous in the 1930s for rescuing people when they found themselves facing danger at the dock in Swansea. Jack, believed to be a black retriever, was never afraid of jumping into the River Tawe when he heard someone call for help, even saving a young boy and an adult swimmer. Jack won several awards for his courageous behaviour, and during his relatively short life of seven years he saved almost thirty people – individuals who otherwise would surely have perished. He is buried in St Helen's Rugby Grounds and even has a pub named in his honour, the once thriving Swansea Jacks. At the start of the new millennium he was awarded the title of 'Dog of the Century', in honour of all the lives he saved.

The grounds of St Helen's.

The Swansea Jack – once a popular pub but now sadly dilapidated.

Barbara Hardy

Although she is perhaps best known for her academic writings on Victorian literature, Barbara Hardy's creative output among other notable works contains a memoir. Entitled *Swansea Girl*, it is a beautifully crafted and evocative reflection of her early life and teenage years in the Welsh city in which she was born and grew up. However, her childhood in 1920s Swansea was not without its difficulties. The daughter of a sailor and a secretary, Hardy experienced what might be termed as the genteel poverty of the lower middle classes first-hand. Passing her eleven-plus exam may have given her access to a grammar school education (at Swansea High School for Girls), but, as was typical for a pupil whose uniform was paid for in instalments, Barbara Hardy understood that in many ways she was different from the majority of her peers. Poverty encouraged her to feel marginalised, and instead of enjoying her intellectual abilities she became all too aware of the social and economic gap that existed between herself and some of the other girls who were taught alongside her. Nevertheless, nothing prevented her academic talents blossoming: she won a place at university and in 1947 was awarded a Batchelor of Arts from the University College of London, followed by a Master of Arts in 1949.

Bombarded by the Blitz

Hardy was particularly adept at writing about the way in which events of the day would impact upon the lives of those who lived through them. Born in 1924, the writer and her own family lived through one of the most momentous events in the whole of Swansea's history, which provided her with infinite detail upon which to draw when writing about the years she spent growing up in Swansea. The event that caused such catastrophe is, of course, Swansea's Blitz, which took place in February 1941.

It is a common misapprehension to believe that only large cities in England, such as Coventry and London, were bombed during the Blitz of the Second World War. Across the skyline of these sprawling metropolises, the Luftwaffe became a terrifying sight, dropping bombs against the wail of sirens as inhabitants frantically scurried to shelters hidden deep beneath the ground. However, in spite of Swansea being relatively small by comparison, its position as a coastal city of one time industrial importance meant that it failed to go unnoticed by the Nazi regime. Over a period of three days, beginning on 19 February 1941 and ending on 21 February 1941, Swansea faced an almost constant bombardment from the skies. It was three of the most frightening days the city and its people had ever faced. Unfortunately, accuracy was not necessarily a strength of the warfare and technology available to the Luftwaffe at the time. Although they aimed mainly at the port and at the coastal region of the city, hoping to destroy the key industrial areas of Swansea, these survived mainly intact. Unfortunately, the same could not be said for the city centre, which is the area the Luftwaffe managed to hit with some accuracy. Shops and streets that had remained standing for years, and were instantly recognisable as representing Swansea's cultural and retail history, simply disappeared overnight. Department stores such as Ben Evans, the ever-popular Victorian market and St Mary's Church were turned into rubble, flattened by the bombs that fell so callously from the sky. Even worse, however, was the loss to human life. In total 230 people lost their lives and over 400 individuals were injured. The inhabitants of post-war Swansea had to contend not only with the grief of devastation and loss, but also the bleakness of a shattered landscape. On looking at the remains of the place he loved, Dylan Thomas is reported to have said, 'Our Swansea is dead.'

However, as both Barbara Hardy and Dylan Thomas both knew only too well, the people of Swansea are courageous and resilient. John Pullen, whose parents managed the Dillwyn Arms pub in Union Street, Swansea, was only twelve at the time of the Blitz in Swansea. Before his death in 2014, he recalled only too well the fear that spread through the city over the course of the three days of attack from the Luftwaffe, and was easily reminded of the scramble for shelter that ensued when bombers flew overhead. However, he remembered the resilience of his neighbours and friends in Union Street and reminisced humorously about the times he and his friends scampered over the wreckage of nearby ruins looking for aeroplane parts he could display in the back of his parent's pub.

It was this tenacity and determination to forge ahead and look towards the future that ensured the people of Swansea were able to unite in order to help rebuild their city after the war was over. The main city centre had to be entirely restructured, the warren of smaller streets and back lanes that harked back to a different era having almost entirely disappeared. The Swansea centre that tourists visit today is almost entirely different to the one they would have visited prior to the Second World War, but in spite of losing something of their history, what the residents of Swansea have gained in the rebuilding of their city centre bears witness to their characteristic courage and good humour.

John Pullen as a young man.

When Academia Beckons

It was against this backdrop of destruction and loss that Barbara Hardy grew up. When she left Swansea to study in London, the city she left behind would never be the same again. Perhaps this was a contributing factor to her decision to never properly return to the city of her childhood. Later, she would buy a cottage on the Gower Peninsula, thus maintaining some links with the area in which she was born; however, her relationship with Swansea itself seems to have been fraught with tension for much of her remaining life. Perhaps she remained disturbed by her memories of school, where she often felt discomfort at never properly fitting in. Or perhaps it was merely that during the 1940s onwards, the academic world in which she yearned to belong seemed to begin and end in London.

Barbara Hardy's academic triumphs were many and varied. She published critical responses to George Eliot, Charles Dickens, Jane Austen and Thomas Hardy among others, as well as writing her memoir and the novel *London Lovers*. As a woman in 1940s and 1950s London, she would no doubt have fought against prejudice, particularly in the academic world. Married and with two children, there will have been those people who would have felt that she should have stayed at home, leaving the ivory towers of university life to men. But if she did face any such pressure, it would have been completely and utterly ignored. Barbara Hardy's roots belonged in a city which had faced great upheaval. If she could live through poverty and the Blitz, there is little doubt that as a writer and an academic she could thrive in an arena that had always previously been male dominated. As an academic scholar and a professor of literature, Barbara Hardy taught at Birbeck and the Royal Holloway, encouraging students to reach their full potential, especially those who had taken more unconventional routes to further education.

Perhaps one of the most fitting awards won by Barbara Hardy is the Rose Mary Crawshay Prize. Awarded to female scholars with initial special preference given to anyone whose essay has links in any way to topics or subject matter associated with Byron, Shelley or Keats, the prize was inaugurated by Lady Crawshay as her way of encouraging women to strive for academic equality. An early follower of the suffrage movement, she used all the resources at her disposal to give working-class women living in the Merthyr and Dowlais area in the mid- to late Victorian period, an opportunity to develop their literacy skills and to help them foster a love of literature. She set up small, free libraries so that working-class people of both genders could access free literature, and encouraged the women who lived in the nearby area to read and discuss the books they read. She realised all too well that for women in particular, social expectation meant that priority was meant to be given to home and hearth. It was almost unforgivable for a woman to neglect the needs of her husband and her own family in preference of her own educational demands. Thus, by setting up the award, Lady Crawshay hoped to readdress this balance and give women a tangible reason for spending their free time, little of it as there might be, dedicated to study. Her prize was started in 1888, and some of its most well-known recipients have included Alice Walker (author of *The Colour Purple*), for her essay submitted in 1954, entitled 'Textual Problems of the First Folio';

Rose Mary Crawshay.

Marilyn Butler (author of *Jane Austen and the War of Ideas*), in 1972 for her essay 'Maria Edgeworth: A Literary Biography' and Penelope Fitzgerald (author of *The Blue Flower*) for her essay submitted in 1984, 'Charlotte Mew and her Friends'. Barbara Hardy won in 1962 for her essay entitled 'The Novels of George Eliot', a subject she was to return to with great success throughout her career. It seems only right that Barbara Hardy, a Swansea-born woman ahead of her time, should be fascinated by another woman, also ahead of her time, who similarly refused to live by the social conventions of the era in which she lived.

Perhaps the best insight into Barbara Hardy's character was written after her death. In her obituary in *The Guardian*, the following was written: 'The literary scholar Barbara Hardy, who has died aged ninety-two, delighted in the challenge of a good argument. Because she never forgot that literature was made from human experience, she was astringently sceptical of theory: particularity and clarity grounded her work.' The human experience that helped strengthen her during her Swansea childhood was also to prove invaluable to her during her knowledge and understanding of literary texts later in life.

DID YOU KNOW?
Barbara Hardy wrote her memoir *Swansea Girl* while staying in a room in the Mackworth Arms Hotel in Swansea. Her father, having left behind his career as a sailor, was a manager at the hotel at the time.

The legacy of Dylan Thomas, Barbara Hardy and Harri Webb lives on in the advice given in this oversized poster in Swansea city centre.

5. 'I Hold a Beast, an Angel and a Madman in Me' (Dylan Thomas)

Tourists and visitors alike to Swansea might perhaps quite rightly expect to find a wide variety of pubs, hotels and wine bars eagerly jostling with one another to capture their business. What they might not expect to find is such a plethora of drinking establishments with such a wide-ranging history. Equally they might be surprised at the number of pubs and hotels with such an interesting catalogue of intriguing stories to share with anyone willing to listen. If you have the time to curl up and listen hard and long enough, your patience will be well rewarded.

The Cross Keys Inn, situated on St Mary's Street, is believed to be one of the oldest pubs in Wales. However, its life as an inn did not begin until the 1600s. From its inception in the fourteenth century, the land on which the Cross Keys was built was used by Bishop de Gower to construct the hospital of Blessed David in 1332. Bishop de Gower was born on the Gower Peninsula and was fortunate indeed to be elected to the role of Archdeacon of St Davids. Typically, anyone other than a Welshman was chosen for this important religious role, but Gower's scholarly, academic record and his time served as chancellor of Oxford University had obviously made a favourable impression on those tasked with choosing the archdeacon to replace Bishop David Martin.

The hospital remained functioning and intact until the early 1400s when in the name of Owain Glyndwr his supporters invaded Swansea, keen to put an end to English rule in Wales. Unfortunately, although their focus was on Swansea Castle, during the ensuing skirmishes parts of the hospital were badly damaged, leading to repair work needing to be carried out.

End of a Healing Era

It was not until 1544 and the Statutes of Edward VI that St David's Hospital, as it now tended to be called, was closed. Under Edward's statutes buildings with Catholic links were dissolved due to Edward's passion for the Protestant religion. With little else to do, the priests who remained on the site of the hospital were forced to make mead. This is the first link with alcohol discovered here, and it is this that connects the modern Cross Keys Inn with traditional brewing. It seems that the monks were successful in their bid to brew and sell alcohol, for in the early part of the twenty-first century as when some foundations were being built on a patch of land near the pub, the remains of an old brewhouse were discovered. It was not until the 1800s that records reveal there to be a registered inn on the site of the Cross Keys, and because of its many historical transformations, it remains a fascinating pub to visit.

St David's Cathedral.

St David's Cathedral.

The Cross Keys pub.

Swansea Castle.

A view of the side entrance to Swansea Castle.

Swansea Castle in all its glory.

Swansea Castle.

The tower at Swansea Castle.

The Mackworth Arms Hotel

Sadly, nothing now remains of the Mackworth Arms Hotel. In spite of the fact that over the years it was in business, its walls and windows witnessed the death of Fanny Imlay, watched Barbara Hardy write her memoir (*Swansea Girl*) and welcomed some famous faces from the world of variety, it has simply vanished from High Street in Swansea. This once prestigious hotel, which even played host to the Emperor Napoleon's nephew, Prince Napoleon Joseph Charles Paul Bonaparte, and his wife Clotilde, who had an overnight stay at the hotel while travelling onwards to Dublin, was initially closed and the building itself knocked down to allow for the siting of Swansea's main post office in 1901. However, the hotel was later rebuilt and flourished for another fifty years.

The hotel is named after the Mackworths, wealthy local industrialists who owned, among other places, the impressive Gnoll Park in Neath. However, the family who owned the hotel were the Jones family, and unlike the Mackworths, they had made their fortune not in industry but through catering. Impressively, the Jones family began with just one café in Cardiff. Their timing, however, was impeccable. Women were beginning to crave 'safe spaces' in which they could enjoy some independence and freedom without worrying about their reputations or their moral standing in front of their families and friends and their husbands in particular. Tearooms and cafés were regarded as the ideal places for women to enjoy some elegant repose, places in which they could meet and chat quite safely. As the nineteenth century drew to a close, the popularity of tearooms and cafés grew. As their marketability blossomed so did the demand for such establishments, especially in larger towns and cities, Swansea being one such place.

For the best part of twenty years, Richard Edwin Jones focussed on building his business and turning a profit through creating cafés and restaurants in and around the Swansea area. This included the tourist areas of Mumbles and Porthcawl, as well as Cardiff, Neath and the centre of Swansea itself. His business flourished, and as it did, so did his desire to build a truly beautiful hotel, one that even the best clients would not shy away from staying in. The original Mackworth Arms Hotel was built on the site covering Nos 41–44 High Street. When it had to be knocked down to accommodate Swansea's post office, there was no way the Jones family intended to allow the hotel's story to end on such a sad note. With a perceptive eye always on future business deals, Richard Edwin Jones ensured that at the time of the Mackworth's closure he bought the rights to the hotel's name and its contents. In this way he was able to secure his family's future business dealings and take the name of their hotel forward.

A New and Luxurious Hotel

When it opened for a second time, the Mackworth Hotel was a luxurious nod to hotel opulence. Every indulgence was catered for, and as an establishment it had surely come a long way from the early 1800s when, as an inn, Fanny Imlay had chosen it as a place not only in which to stay but also in which to take her own life.

A Bradshaw's *Guide to Glamorganshire* from the early twentieth century recommends the Mackworth Hotel as one of the two best places to stay in Swansea – the other being the Castle Hotel. Of Swansea, it tells its readership,

> This important seat of the copper trade, is also a parliamentary borough, (one member), jointly with Neath, etc., and stands at the head of a fine bay, on the west side of Glamorganshire, 216 miles from London by the Great Western and South Wales Railways, population, 41, 606 ... A castle was built here by the Normans, of which a massive quadrangular tower remains, and presents an object of some beauty. Beneath it is the Post Office, a building in the mediaeval style, recently erected. A large Market House built in 1830 is 320 feet long. There are three churches, the only one deserving of notice is the parish church of St Mary, which was rebuilt in the last century. Some of the numerous chapels are well built.

Apart from the guide's slightly sceptical view of the religious edifices of Swansea, this is, on the whole, a positive introduction to the city and one which would undoubtedly attract tourists to the area. It would therefore be particularly pleasing for the Mackworth Hotel's owners to see their establishment so highly recommended to prospective tourists.

In keeping with the opulence and charm of the refurbished hotel, it also attracted tourists of the more well-known variety. Famous guests to stay at the Mackworth included American film stars Laurel and Hardy, and the Second World War *Forces Sweetheart* Dame Vera Lynne.

Until the 1950s the Mackworth Arms remained an important part of Swansea life, providing tourists with a place to say, function rooms for wedding receptions and local gatherings, and bedrooms that were suitable for even the most celebrated of guests. Its demise and demolition at the end of the 1950s signalled an end of an era not just in Swansea and the surrounding area but also perhaps in the type of luxury accommodation that in post-war Britain, was simply too expensive for the majority of tourists.

Wind Street

Swansea's Wind Street currently plays an important part in the nightlife of Swansea. Running through the heart of the city centre, it is filled on both sides of the street with bars, clubs, restaurants and pubs. On weekends a cacophony of noise can be heard echoing from its entrance opposite Castle Square as students, locals and tourists (many of them stags and hens on weekends away) party and unwind into the early hours of the morning. However, Wind Street did not always provide such a raucous nightlife. Indeed, throughout its existence it has been a mixture of retail and residential buildings, as well as the traditional pubs it is now so frequently associated with. A glance through time proves that the history of Wind Street is really rather intriguing.

Historians believe Wind Street, although now a Mecca for the modern and the young, could be as old as a thousand years and that its routes can be traced back as far as Norman

Wind Street.

times. In other words, Wind Street could be as old as Swansea Castle. This means that Wind Street would very much have been a working environment with traditional crafts such as leatherwork and weaving – the goods people at the time relied so heavily upon – being made and sold from the very premises families lived in. The atmosphere would have been very much like a market. Picture a scene with cramped wooden houses covered with a mixture of dung, mud and straw so that the inhabitants would be kept dry and warm in the winter months, animals roaming the street, children playing, women cooking over an open fire, and men selling their wares on the spaces outside their homes, and you have a very good example of what life was like for the early settlers who made their home on Wind Street.

Nothing really changed in Wind Street for several hundred years. It retained its importance as a residential and retail hub, with local residents visiting the street to buy crafts and merchandise from the people who made their homes and set up their business on the street. In the sixteenth century, a market and later an important yearly fair took place on Wind Street. These were important as they encouraged trade from further

An old residential building that once belonged to a surgeon who lived on Wind Street.

afield and became responsible for securing the economy of not just Wind Street but also Swansea itself. It was also probably due to the weekly market and the annual fairs that ale was first sold on a large commercial basis on Wind Street. Certainly, as the century passed, alehouses began to spring up along the side of the street, although Wind Street very much remained a diverse street with a competitive mixture of residential abodes and shops running along each street side.

There was also something pleasingly egalitarian about Wind Street. As the years passed, it retained its healthy mix of residents, so there was nothing surprising for visitors to the street to note that those members of classes, such as surgeons and physicians, would be living next door to those from the lower ranks, such as sailors. Wind Street also continued to remain pleasingly diverse in the range of trade and retail outlets it offered. As well as providing inns and hotels in which visitors could rest themselves and their horses, the street provided a pharmacist, various banks and a clockmaker's shop.

Gradually, as the retail side of Wind Street became more and more successful, the residential homes became vacated as fewer and fewer people chose to live there. During the Victorian period, however, more and more shops decided to choose Wind Street as the base from which they would trade. Some of them were quite prestigious and the street flourished – both economically and because of the number of people who visited on a daily basis.

Known by some as 'the Harrods of Wales', the Ben Evans department store was to shopping what the Mackworth Hotel was to the tourist trade. Pampering to its every shopper's need, the Ben Evans store came complete with nearly forty different departments, a hairstylists and a lady's refreshment room. Standing proudly on the cusp of Wind Street, doormen in smart uniforms stood to attention, waiting to help guests in and out of the building. Shoppers came from all over west Wales, and sometimes from even further afield, to experience shopping in such opulent and luxurious surroundings and to have their every whim catered for. The store served Swansea and its customers extremely well until tragedy struck during the three-day Blitz of 1941. The department store was all but destroyed, and a huge part of both Swansea and Wind Street's retail history was gone forever.

From one Extreme to the Other

This does not mean, however, that the whole of Wind Street had gone completely upmarket. There were still reports of drunken behaviour to be read about in the local newspapers. On 16 June 1893, for example, the *South Wales Daily Post* headlines on page 3 with the story of 'The Missing Glais Furnace Man'. According to the report in the *Post*, he was last seen in Wind Street. However, his body was later discovered by Police Constable Tasker in the waters of the South Dock in Swansea. Details of the inquest as reported in the newspaper are as follows:

David Rees, a glass furnace man said the deceased was his brother. He was an unmarried man of twenty-five years of age. He and his brother arrived at Swansea about one o'clock on Saturday, and with some friends they went for an afternoon trip in the Alexandria. They came onshore shortly after five o'clock , and with the exception of the deceased , they went into a cook shop in Wind Street. His brother, accompanied by another man, went up the street, and this was the last they saw of him.

The journalists were well placed to write such reports as several local papers now had their offices on Wind Street itself. From as early as 1804, *The Cambrian*, owned in part by Lewis Weston Dillwyn, had been started from offices on the street itself, and later they were followed by the *South Wales Daily Post*. Just as today, the newspaper filed reports of drunken, bawdy behaviour and acts of petty revenge and violence, all apparently made worse by the alcohol that had been consumed while the injured parties enjoyed some light refreshment on Wind Street.

Up until the latter years of the twentieth century it was still possible to find a bank on Wind Street, but now these too have disappeared. The street boasts one or two corner shops, but other than these small, intimate retail experiences Wind Street's fame lies in its reputation for non-stop clubbing and partying. A well-known stop on the tourist map, it is the place to visit if alcohol is needed, or if a visitor needs to let their hair down. However, while taking a sip of white wine or a sup of John Smith's beer, it is interesting to ponder on Wine Street's past and to consider the millions of footsteps that have trodden upon the street's winding surfaces in its thousand-year history.

DID YOU KNOW?
Salubrious Passage, a narrow alleyway leading off Wind Street into Salubrious Place, appear from their photograph to be rather ironically named! There is some disagreement as to why such places would be blessed with such names, although one argument is that Salubrious Place gives a very fine view if the beach and so early tourists to Swansea, wishing to escape the noise, chaos and smell of Wind Street, might therefore find the passageway a refreshing one, regardless of its appearance.

Salubrious Passage.

Traditional light in Salubrious Place.

Salubrious Place with Salubrious Passage just behind it.

Dylan Thomas and Swansea Pubs – Reality or Myth?

It would be impossible to do full justice to any chapter concerning pubs in Swansea without mentioning the writer and poet Dylan Thomas. The fact that he is almost as well known for his drinking as for his writing might be an uncomfortable truth, but it is one that is difficult to get away from, particularly as his early and untimely death at the age of thirty-nine in New York on 9 November 1953 is so often associated with alcohol abuse.

Of one of his favourite tipples, Thomas once wrote, 'I liked the taste of beer, its live white lather, its brass-bright depths, the sudden world through the wet brown world of the glass, the tilted rush to the lips and the slow-swallowing down to the lapping belly, the salt on the tongue, the foam at the corners.' Such beautiful words to describe an alcoholic beverage surely show that the writer had a remarkable appreciation for the brew that he sipped. One of his favourite pubs to give him his earliest experience of beer was the Uplands Tavern, located not far from his home on Cwmdonkin Drive. It was his local, renowned then as now for being the sort of old-fashioned pub that Dylan Thomas loved to drink in. He even had his favourite place to sit, a warm snug, from where he could watch the rest of the world go by.

Like many artistic young men of the 1930s, Dylan Thomas was a bohemian, someone who loved to surround himself with fellow writers, artists and poets. In Swansea, the place for such a band of people to meet was the Kardomah Café on Castle Street. Here, surrounded by poets such as Vernon Watkins and Charles Fisher, the composer Daniel

The Uplands Tavern.

Jones and artists Alfred Janes and Mabley Owen, Dylan Thomas loved to hold court, discussing the culture and politics of the day while sipping coffee and smoking cigarettes. Sadly, the Kardomah fell victim to the German bombardment of the early 1940s, the Luftwaffe flattening it to ruins in the Blitz. One more of Dylan's precious Swansea landmarks had disappeared, but this time not forever. The Kardomah's owners, in a display of spirit so typical of Swansea folk, simply reopened in new premises. The café is still flourishing today, serving customers traditional fare, its waiters and waitresses neatly turned out in crisp black and white uniforms. It is an homage to the Swansea of Dylan Thomas's youth and to an era of politeness and customer service of which Mrs Thomas would surely have approved.

A picture of Dylan Thomas outside the Uplands Tavern.

The Kardomah Coffee Shop.

No Sign but Plenty of Wine

There were times, of course, when Dylan and his band of followers required something stronger than the coffee that they loved to sip in the Kardomah Café. When this happened, the group of bohemians would very often move round the corner from Castle Street to Wind Street and to one of Swansea's oldest pubs, the No Sign Wine Bar, or the No Sign as it was more typically known. With parts of the building dating back to the fourteenth century, Dylan Thomas and his friends had a particular soft spot for the pub, so much so that it is believed to appear in Thomas' short story *The Followers* under the guise of the Wine Vaults: 'A man with a balloon tied to his cap pushed a shrouded barrow up a dead end. A baby with an ancient face sat in its pram outside the wine vaults, quiet, very wet, peering cautiously all round it. It was the saddest evening I had ever known.'

DID YOU KNOW?
In keeping with its tradition of literary discussions and following on from the conversations begun by Dylan Thomas, Vernon Watkins and their No Sign Wine Bar continues to be a place of culture in Swansea. It still regularly holds poetry readings, and is especially welcoming to new and up-and-coming poets.

An artist's illustration of Salubrious Passage and how it would have looked in 1876.

An artist's illustration of the No Sign Bar and how it would have looked in 1690.

6. Copperopolis – An Industrialists' Extravaganza

The Industrial Revolution remains historically complex and in some ways controversial. On the one hand it brought prosperity and much needed employment to large towns and cities, providing economic security to areas of undeniable deprivation. However, on the other hand, the Industrial Revolution brought with it a plethora of problems, interestingly both economical as well as social, and its impact on Swansea was no different than it was on any other town or city across Great Britain. Even writers and political commentators who spoke at the time were aware of the difficulties that were being posed by the new influx of technology. They were also well aware that as much as the arrival of factories and ironworks created employment, they also created social problems on a tragic scale.

The London-based writer Charles Dickens was one of the first and most predominant people to come to the aid of the workers who were forced to seek employment in the often dangerous and usually depressing new places of work that were sprouting around Britain. He also acknowledged the fact that the factory owners, pit managers and iron masters who could take advantage of the new business methods now in place were keen to make money and less keen to worry about providing a decent wage or safe working conditions for their employees. With no set regulations in place, it was easy for unscrupulous owners to turn a blind eye to hazardous working conditions, or to the fact that many of their workers were obviously under age and would have been better served going to school. But times were hard, and Dickens was one of the many with a more philanthropic view to realise that some parents had no choice but to send their children to work. They needed the extra income however small it was, and however much danger had to be faced in order to earn it.

Hard Times for All

Dickens used his novel *Hard Times* as a vehicle by which he could express his horror at the way workers were treated, particularly those who worked for unscrupulous masters who cared nothing for their employees. The problem stemmed from the fact that they believed those who worked for them to be easily replaceable. Dickens' novel *Hard Times* truly captures the brutality of the working man and woman's everyday regime at this time and allows Dickens to be scathing in his response to men such as Bounderby, who employ many locals and treat them as machines instead of human beings with feelings and souls. Indeed, such is Bounderby's lack of humanity that he regards his workers as 'Hands', tools who are there to do a job but who are devoid of human emotion and therefore can be treated as machines who can be expected to work all hours of the day and night for little payment without it reflecting badly on Mr Bounderby's position as a stalwart of the local area. In Chapter Five of *Hard Times* Dickens describes the industrial town of Coketown, focusing on the huge factory towers that dominate the town, believing that their strings of smoke are serpents, trailing into the sky. However, he could just as easily have been describing Swansea, or any other town or city caught in the throes of the Industrial Revolution.

> Coketown, to which Messrs Bounderby and Gradgrind now walked, was a triumph of fact; it had no greater taint of fancy in it than Mrs Gradd herself. Let us strike the key-note, Coke-town, before pursuing our tune. It was a town of red brick, or of brick that would have been red if the smoke and ashes had allowed it; but, as matters stood it was a town of unnatural red and black like the painted face of a savage. It was a town of machinery and tall chimneys, out of which interminable serpents of smoke trailed themselves forever and ever, and never got uncoiled. It had a black canal in it and a river that ran purple will ill-smelling dye, and vast piles of building full of windows where there was a rattling and a trembling all day long, and where the piston of the steam-engine worked monotonously up and down, like the head of an elephant in a state of melancholy madness. It contained several large streets all very like one another, and many small streets , still more like one another, inhabited by people equally like one another, who all went in and out at the same hours, with the same sound upon the same pavements, to do the same work, and to whom every day was the same as yesterday and tomorrow, and e year the counterpart of the last and the next. These attributes of Coketown were in the main inseparable from the work by which it was sustained, against them were to be set off, comforts of life which their way all over the world, and elegancies of life which made, we will not ask how much of the fine lady, who could not bear to hear the place mentioned.

Here, Dickens's beautiful yet brutal description of life in Coketown is a perfectly realised vignette of life in an industrial town or city. From Swansea to Salford, and Cumbria to Cardiff, those workers unfortunate to experience life in a pit or a factory, such as the one owned by Bounderby, or a copper works, such as the ones next to the River Tawe in Swansea, knew what it was like to have their lives stripped of all individuality. Their masters did not care about their personal dreams or future plans; they cared only if their workers turned up on time and in a suitable state for work. Such employers were mere ghosts, men and women and sometimes even children, whose lives reflected those of everyone else in their place of work. There was no time for idle chat or daydreaming, no time for worry or illness. Their lives were strictly regimented and they worked as if they themselves were part machine, too afraid to admit to illness, too scared to moan about pain. Employment was hard to come by and no one could afford to be out of work. Interestingly, although it is often believed that disabled people were given little recourse to work in times gone by and that they were kept hidden from view, this wasn't typically always the case. People with disabilities or who had been maimed at work were no different to anyone else in that they could ill afford to be unemployed. They had to learn, however, to be more resourceful than anyone else. Replacement limbs made from wood were often used as were crutches to lean upon. Economic necessity meant they were forced to work, as sick pay as the concept we know today simply didn't exist. Furthermore, there were times when the owners of the industrial works need as many 'hands' as possible to complete the task being undertaken. In those situations, the uninformed stigma we associate with attitudes towards disability of 150–200 years ago simply ceased to exist.

In *Hard Times* the character of Stephen Blackpool represents everyman, the typical hardworking employee who wants nothing more than to earn his money and return home when at last he is allowed out of the factory gates. Unwilling to enter into the politics of joining a union, he also declines Mr Bounderby's request to spy on his fellow workers, thus leaving himself an outcast and at the mercy of two opposing sides who are willing to hurt those who do not support their particular beliefs. In a time of desperation, Stephen turns to God, but he faces a lonely death when he falls down an unkempt mineshaft.

Once again Dickens highlights two problems that were faced by Swansea workers as well as workers all over the country. The difficulty of whether or not to join a union was always problematic. Having somewhere to turn when there were difficulties at work has always been considered the right thing to do, but joining a union in the nineteenth century was not always as straightforward as it is today. Union membership could bring extra hardship form employers who disagreed with them, and this in turn led to skirmishes and violent outbreaks. The matter of poor health and safety regulations was also a difficulty that raised its head time and time again. No matter how many workers were killed from poorly closed mine shafts or badly maintained machinery, managers were reluctant to spend money on such concerns, believing their money was better spent on themselves. It is interesting to note as well that near the end of the extract from *Hard Times*, Dickens writes about the 'fine ladies' who enjoy buying the goods made at the factory, but would prefer not to be reminded of the place where the items were made. As usual, Dickens makes a comment that manages to transcend time, for this is the equivalent of twenty-first-century shoppers ignoring the sweatshops where their 'fast fashion' has been stitched together – often by children as young as eight.

Swansea – a Key Player in the Industrial South

Geographically, Swansea was in a prime place to take advantage of all the elements that were needed if an area was going to be of prime importance in the Industrial Revolution. Although it was not large, Swansea was near the sea, and the River Tawe flowed through it. It could thereby use nearby ports to its advantage as well as water from the river, which could be pumped to the nearby works that soon started to be built along the side of the Tawe. Swansea could also take advantage of the nearby coal mines. This was useful as coal is an imperative ingredient when smelting copper ore from the ore itself. Before long, the copper industry was booming in Swansea and it soon became known as 'Copperopolis', easily able to use its ports to export its copper from the smelting works in Swansea to countries all over the world. However, with money comes greed. In spite of the fact that the owners of the copper works were becoming exceedingly rich off the hard work of the people who toiled for them, they wanted more money with which to line their pockets. The 1840s in Swansea was a particularly aggressive time with violent outbreaks and clashes occurring between the masters and their men. One of the most unpopular legislations involved the charging of tolls to pass through Swansea itself. It was one thing to pay money to pass through Swansea's gates, but quite another to expect

The River Tawe.

The River Tawe flowing past Swansea's Liberty Stadium.

A statue recognising the achievements of Sir Henry Hussey Vivian, son of John Henry Vivian, both Swansea industrialists.

people to pay the Turnpike Trust to cross along its roads and byroads. As tempers frayed the violence escalated, leading to the burning of Ty Coch Gate. To add insult to injury, several months later the wages of the workers were cut, leaving them little choice but to go on strike. As stubborn as they remained, there was no way the workers could continue to live without a regular income, something their canny if callous employers knew only too well. After five weeks the workers had no choice but to return to work. It must have been in a state of great bitterness that they entered the work's gate on that first day back. They had been unsuccessful in their efforts to increase or even restore their pay. They had lost five week's wages and worse still, John Henry Vivian, one of the owners of the works whose employers were known to have gone on strike, blacklisted those who had taken part in any of the outbursts and skirmishes. Vivian was not an employer known for his compassion or for his belief in the rights of everyday workers.

The inscription on Sir Henry Hussey Vivian's statue.

Running out of Space

As the Industrial Revolution swept across Swansea, one of the things that happened that reflected events elsewhere was a devastating housing shortage. Despite the fact that at the start of the nineteenth century Swansea was relatively small, with a population of approximately 20,000, it began to find it difficult to cope with the influx of people who arrived looking for work. Migrant workers came from relatively near (such as the rural farming areas of Carmarthen, whose workers were struggling to make a profit or to find work that paid enough from which they could make a decent living) and from further afield in Britain or even Europe. They arrived in a desperate bid to find work. However, what they also needed to find was a place to live, particularly if they brought a family with them. As a result accommodation became cramped, with large families forced to live, eat and sleep in one room. Areas such as Bethesda Court, Ebenezer Street and York Street became synonymous with poor sanitation, pollution and cramped, poorly built houses. Outdoor toilets ended up being shared by, on average, fifty individuals, and cholera outbreaks struck in 1832 and 1849. It was not until 1854, after the physician John

The River Tawe and the ruins of Copperopolis.

Snow completed studying the water pump in Broad Street, Soho, London, following a devastating outbreak of cholera that killed over 600 people that bad sanitation and infected drinking water were understood to be the reasons why people caught and died from the disease. Therefore, for several years Swansea was at the mercy of ill-informed medical men who knew very little about why their patients were dying.

The situation was not helped by the existing owners of homes trying to make money from this new influx of arrivals. Very often they would force their family into one bedroom so that they could rent out the remaining room to a worker and his family. This often resulted in at least ten people sharing one small two-up two-down terraced house. It instantly became a breeding ground for germs, with infections and diseases passing easily from one family member to the next.

It was not until competitors from foreign climes began to compete favourably with Swansea that the decline of the city's industrial revolution began. By the end of the nineteenth century, industry as Swansea had known it had all but disappeared. Only some ruins of the copper works remained, with its bricks scarring the side of the River Taff, left as a constant reminder of Swansea's once thriving industrial past.

Not much is now left of Swansea's once illustrious industrious past.

Where once the River Tawe was surrounded by industry, trees now flank its sides.

7. From the Rake to the Riddle

Swansea is a coastal city. Throughout its history, money has been made as surely as the tides have swept in and out of the bay, and ships have sailed in and out of its ports bringing news from far-flung countries, spices and silks from the east, and fish from the west. With just as much certainty, however, the waves have roared in anger, skies that were blue have turned to pewter grey and a sea that once seemed warm and inviting has turned to icy-grey anger. Lives have been lost, and lives have been found. The sea is an unforgiving mistress, and for every life found there have always been ten times as many lost. Lost to the bitter clutches of a jealous and tormented strip of water that never fails to surprise and to shock those who sail upon her.

The stories surrounding the shipwrecks that have occurred around Swansea Bay, Mumbles and the Gower Peninsula are at once terrifying and tragic, underlying once and for all the flippant nature of the sea to which the area is in many ways beholden. Perhaps this is highlighted more than ever by the alarming story of the *Helvetia*.

Helvetia

Standing on the beach at Rhossili on a calm summer's day, it seems impossible to believe that this part of the Gower could ever be responsible for shipwrecks and accidents at sea. Yet, return on a blustery day with the wind catching the waves and spinning them into an angry maelstrom, and it seems entirely possible.

Looking down from the cliffs overlooking the beach at Rhossili, it is possible to see that when the tide is out the flatness of the sand is scarred by several jagged wooden posts that stick up at odd angles. These posts are all that are left of the *Helvetia*, a wooden boat carrying timber to be purchased by the merchants of Swansea. Unfortunately, on 1 November 1887, it fell victim to the wild gales that were causing havoc at sea throughout the day and night. The captain of the *Helvetia* planned to dock along with another ship, also carrying timber, at Swansea Dock, but the fierce winds and waves made this impossible. The two ships were literally storm-tossed and faced the very real possibility of being thrown completely off course and down through the Bristol Channel. The captain of the *Helvetia*'s companion ship managed to find safety and shelter on Lundy Island, but those on board the *Helvetia* were not so lucky. After the ship skidded across Helwick Sands, the wind blew it into Rhossili Bay, where the sea was not deep enough to carry the *Helvetia*; shipwreck seemed inevitable. Fortunately, using all the might of the crew on board, the captain managed to finally drop anchor at Rhossili before being rescued by the coastguard – men who bravely risked their lives to save him. In spite of the danger involved for his crew, however, the captain was loathe to simply abandon the *Helvetia* and give it up to the power of the sea. Its cargo of wood was expensive, and losing it would mean economic difficulties further down the line. Bearing in mind the

Swansea Bay looking towards the Mumbles.

The cliffs at Rhossili.

The beach at Rhossili on a quiet day.

Three Cliffs Bay from the sea.

The wreck of the Helvetia.

stories he had heard of looters and smugglers, the captain made the decision to try to salvage as much of the wood as he possibly could. He therefore broke the news to his men that they were to stay on board the damaged ship and guard their precious cargo until further help could be called for. Mother Nature, however, had ideas of her own, and as usual both the weather and the sea refused to be controlled. The men on board ship had no choice but to abandon their vessel when the anchor began to disappear and they risked drowning along with their precious cargo as the ship began to slip beneath the rough and unforgiving waves of the Atlantic Ocean. Finally the men were allowed to abandon wreckage and head to shore.

Further Disaster

The following day, when the tide was low, the true extent of the damage could be assessed. The *Helvetia* was now a tangled mess – unrecognisable as the ship the men had sailed in, and certainly unsalvageable. Over the next few weeks, the men collected all the timber they could save and the captain gave instructions for it to be sold at auction. Here it was bought cheaply by the timber merchants of south Wales, all eager for a bargain. Unfortunately, it was when the final load of timber was being cleared from the wreck and distributed that tragedy struck.

Boats from the local area, including Mumbles and Llanelli, were used to carry the timber from Rhossili. Problems occurred when the boats were caught in shallow waters due to the low tide. Although they were successfully rescued, one of the anchors that had been used to stabilise the boats got left behind. Local men were paid to attach it to one of the buoys at sea so that it could be kept safely until collected later when the boat made its return journey. This did not happen until a few months later. However, the boat that was used was not strong enough to hold the six men sent to relinquish the anchor, along with the anchor itself. Despite the calmness of the conditions, this tragedy had more to do with human error than Mother Nature. Poor calculations regarding weight resulted in the boat capsizing and all but one man losing his life. The sea and the wreck of the *Helvetia* had finally claimed their first victims. Their watery graves are marked by the wooden posts that jut eerily out of the sand, and as the sea continually washes over them they too are in danger of disappearing forever – as lost as the souls whose lives were claimed by a determined and all-powerful sea.

The Rake and the Riddle

This is a common enough phrase to be heard in Swansea and its surrounding coastal area. Indeed, there is now even a restaurant on Gower called the Rake and Riddle. What is less well known, however, is what exactly a rake and riddle are used for. A rake is pronged and is used to scrape away the sand in order to search for cockles along the beach. The rather strangely named riddle is a sieve, and is used to separate the cockles from the sand and other unwanted debris. Tradition has it that until quite recently searching for cockles was always a woman's job, and indeed the many stories involving women combing the beach in search of cockles to sell seems to support this. It is literally back-breaking work, involving bending over the sand for hours at a time, searching for enough cockles to fill a bucket and turn a profit. However, at one point in time this was one of the only ways

The Lougher Estuary.

available for women who lived near the coast, particularly in rural areas across the Gower Peninsula to contribute to the economy of family life. It could also be dangerous and difficult work, meaning that sometimes lives could be lost just as easily by working on the sand as they could be by working on the sea.

The problem occurred because while women were busy cockle picking, they could be caught out so easily by the tide, suddenly finding themselves stranded and cut off from the shore. In order to stay warm, the women always wrapped thoroughly in layer upon layer of clothing, which often made it difficult for them to escape quickly, particularly once the sea began to lap at their feet. One of Swansea's newspapers, *The Cambrian*, in an article dated 6 July 1906, captured perfectly the danger the women of Swansea faced:

> Cockle Women In Danger. Surrounded By The Tide At Loughor Sands. An exciting scene was witnessed on Friday morning at the Loughor Sands. Two cockle-women were returning home heavily laden, when to their surprise, they were surrounded on each side by the tide. Their shrieks were heard far away, and at once a man, working at Loughor Bridge, Launched a boat and rescued the terrified women.

However, unfortunately not all cockle pickers were as lucky as the women in this news story. Elizabeth Dallimore was one such fatality. She drowned along with a friend in 1937, caught out by a quickly paced tide, one which has no patience to wait for man nor woman as it endeavours to race across the shore.

Independence, but at a Price

Penclawdd has long been the area of Swansea that has been most associated with cockle picking, but it is here that the social condition of women seemed at times to be upside down when compared to the rest of Swansea society. For the most part, the lives of local men and women reflected the typical structure of society, particularly throughout the whole of the nineteenth century and up to the middle of the twentieth century. At these particular times, men were also regarded as the main source of income in a household. If possible, when the job situation allowed, they were the ones who brought economic stability to the household. A woman might contribute by taking in sewing or laundry, but her main role was as a caregiver. She was meant to look after the family, to cook and clean, to nurture and to help stabilise the moral welfare of her family. In Penclawdd, however, something slightly different began to happen and with this came a woman's opportunity for social and economic freedom at a time when this was most assuredly unheard of. As a cockle picker, a woman could do more than simply support the household in times of need or when her husband was sick or unemployed. She could actually become its main source of income, earning more than it was possible for her husband to earn. Not only could she pick the cockles, however, but she would also be responsible for taking them to market and selling them. Thus, she also ruled over the commercial aspect of her small business empire. It must never be forgotten that this independence came at a cost, however. Cockle picking was hard and dangerous work. The women needed to be constantly on guard for the reckless actions of a perilous sea.

View of Penclawdd village overlooking the estuary.

Penclawdd village.

The fast-moving tide of the Lougher Estuary.

The vast expanse of the Lougher Estuary proved a danger to many cockle women.

Swansea Canal, an integral part of the city's industrial past.

Swansea Canal.

Swansea Canal. Note the juxtaposition of Swansea's past alongside its present in the form of a new housing estate.

Swansea Canal.

The Hafod – Morfa Copperworks, Swansea.

Hafod –Morfa Copperworks.

The HAFOD-MORFA Copperworks
Gwaith Copr HAFOD MORFA

Entrance to the Hafod Works

THE main entry point to the Hafod works was provided by this gateway, which workers accessed via a bridge over the Swansea Canal. Many of the workers lived in nearby Trevivian or Vivian's Town (now Hafod), a settlement along the Neath Road built in stages by the Vivian family from 1837 onwards. The canal bridge has been built over and become hidden in recent years but remains of the canal are to be found close to this spot. Also to be found nearby is the Works' Office (now Landore Social Club) and a lime kiln built during the mid-nineteenth century. The kiln is the last of 54 limekilns that once stood alongside the Swansea Canal. Wagon-loads of limestone were pushed up a ramp and emptied in from the top of the kiln. Unlike many other kilns of this time, the lime produced was used for building and not agricultural purposes. The limestone came to the Hafod Copperworks from Mumbles via the Oystermouth Railway and Swansea Canal.

Mynedfa Gwaith yr Hafod

Y PORTH hwn oedd y brif fynedfa i Waith yr Hafod, a byddai'r gweithwyr yn ei gyrraedd ar bont dros Gamlas Abertawe. Roedd llawer o'r gweithwyr yn byw gerllaw yn Nhrevivian (Yr Hafod bellach), anheddiad o adeiladwyd yn raddol ar hyd Ffordd Castell Nedd gan y teulu Vivian o 1837 ymlaen. Adeiladwyd dros bont y gamlas a'i chuddio yn ystod y blynyddoedd diwethaf hyn, ond erys gweddillion y gamlas i'w gweld gerllaw. Ys yn yr ardal gellir gweld hefyd hen Swyddfa'r Gwaith Copr (Clwb Cymdeithasol Glandŵr bellach) ac odyn galch a godwyd tua chanol y bedwaredd ganrif ar bymtheg. Dyma'r un olaf o 54 o odynau calch a safai unwaith ar hyd Gamlas Abertawe. Byddai gwageneidiau o garreg galch yn cael eu gwthio i fyny esgynfa a'u dadlwytha i mewn trwy ben uchaf yr odyn. Yn wahanol i lawer o odynau ar yr adeg, ar gyfer adeiladu yn hytrach nag i ddibenion amaethyddol y cynhyrchid y galch yma. Deuai'r garreg galch i Waith Copr yr Hafod o'r Mwmbwls ar hyd Rheilffordd Ystumllwynarth a Chamlas Abertawe.

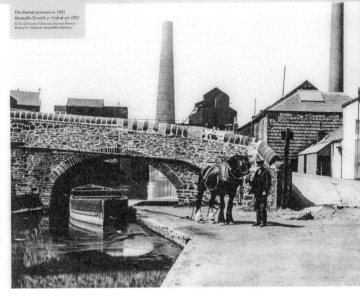

The Hafod entrance in 1931
Mynedfa Gwaith yr Hafod ym 1931

Original door and metal work in early 1980s / Drws a gwaith metal gwreiddiol ar ddechrau'r 1980au

Above: An image of how the copperworks would once have looked.

Right: Further ruins of the copperworks.

A tribute to those who worked at the copperworks.

The copperworks.

Modern-day Swansea, the Meridian Tower.

DID YOU KNOW?
The women who picked cockles did so in bare feet. Regardless of the weather, they walked across the sand with nothing to protect their feet.

Not only did the women pick cockles in their bare feet, but when ready to sell their wares, they also walked most of the way to Swansea's commercial centre in bare feet, stopping a short distance away to put on their shoes in order to look presentable.

Acknowledgements

Thank you to the Pullen family for allowing me to use the memories of John Pullen and his recollections of his time in the Blitz. Thank you to Nigel Pullen for his beautiful photography and to Nigel Pullen and Morgan Tippings for their technical assistance.

Thank you, as always, to my family – who knew that a whole world could fit so snugly inside a city?